SPLIT INK

I ♥ MICHAEL BALL

& OTHER PLAYS

By Alexander Millington

Published by Playdead Press 2022

© Alexander Millington 2022

Alexander Millington has asserted his rights under the Copyright, Design and Patents Act, 1988, to be identified as the author of this work.

A CIP catalogue record for this book is available from the British Library.

ISBN 978-1-910067-96-3

Playdead Press
www.playdeadpress.com

I Heart Michael Ball was first performed at The Old Joint Stock Theatre, Birmingham on 26 May 2022 with the following cast:

ALEX   Alexander Millington

GEORGE   Harry Cocking

Director   Helen Millington
Additional Direction   Alexander Millington

The production was supported using public funding by the National Lottery through Arts Council England.

Alexander Millington | Writer/Performer

Alexander is Creative Director of Split Infinitive, devising and writing all previous performances. Alexander's theatrical credits includes *Three Way* (2021/22 Tour), *The Impossible Dream* (The Stockwell Playhouse's One Act Play Festival), *The Understudies* (2016 Tour) and *The Concept of Love* (2012 & 2016). Alexander has also had work broadcast on BBC Radio including *A Real Christmas* (2020). Alexander is a Licentiate of Trinity College London and holds an MA in Playwriting from the University of Lincoln. Alexander is acknowledged in the True Acting Institutes *Best Ten Minute Plays of 2019* for his play, *Window Shopping.* He has also collaborated on works with the American Dramatist Guild and New Works Playhouse for online performances of his work *Cigarettes & Chairs* (2021) and *For Better or For Worse* (2020).

Helen Millington | Director

Helen is Artistic Director of Split Infinitive, directing their previous performances. Helen has been directing, performing and producing theatre for 25 years and, as such, has gained extensive experience in a wide variety of performance related fields. She has previously performed with the Lincoln Shakespeare Company, in The Lincoln

Mystery Plays, as Titania in a national tour of *A Midsummer Night's Dream* and has directed various productions including devised performances and children's theatre. Alongside Split Infinitive, Helen runs Lincoln School of Speech and Drama, is Secretary of The Lincoln Music & Drama Festival, spent several years as Head of Speech and Drama at Stamford Endowed Schools, and has adjudicated many poetry competitions. She is a member of the Society of Teachers of Speech and Drama and holds an MA in Contemporary British Theatre from the School of Fine and Performing Art at the University of Lincoln. Through Split Infinitive, Helen has also previously worked on R&D sessions for projects including *Three Way* (2021), *I am an actor...* (2020), *Over Time* (2020) *Jump, Jump, Push* (2019), *New Year, Same Me* (2019), and *Child's Play* (2018).

SPLIT INFINITIVE

Split Infinitive is a Lincolnshire based theatre company dedicated to creating original theatre, which explores the dynamics between spectator and performer and examines the relationships created throughout our lives. Established in 2019, Split Infinitive has worked with local and emerging artists whilst developing new work. Since 2019, they have collaborated with other theatre companies to create engaging online performances including two performances broadcast on BBC Radio (*A Real Christmas* and *Over Time*). In 2021, they produced their first touring production, *Three Way* which toured to the Camden and Greater Manchester Fringe Festivals, as well as being part of De Montfort University's LGBT+ Creative Voices: Poetry, Monologues, Music & Memoir for LGBT+ History Month in 2022. *I Heart Michael Ball* is Split Infinitive's first Arts Council England supported production and toured to the Brighton, Bedford and Camden Fringe Festivals, Offbeat Festival in Oxford and a variety of other venues across the country.

Twitter | @SplitTheatre
Facebook | SplitInfinitiveTheatre
Instagram | SplitInfinitiveTheatre
www.splitinfinitivetheatre.co.uk

Acknowledgements

Special thanks go to;

Lewis Ranshaw for his amazing photography throughout the rehearsal process and making an excellent body and voice double for our trailer.

Graham Lowes for technical support with online material and for his camera work on our trailers.

And to all the people who kindly donated to our funding page and attended our scripted performances whilst we developed the script: Mary-Jane Ives, Oliver Marshall, Julie Whiting, Mike 'The Fox' Belcher, Sarah Baishaw, Alex Baishaw, Lucy Housego, Andy Jordan, Angela Wood, Karen Barrett, Mack Ranshaw, Kathy Ashwin and Ruthie Whiting.

Contents:

I Heart Michael Ball

Alexander Millington

CHARACTERS

Alex, *unspecified gender*

George, *male, Alex's brother*

I Heart Michael Ball is written as a monologue performance with all characters being performed by the person playing Alex. For the 2022 production, which coincides with this publication, we made the directorial decision that the character of George would be performed by a second actor, his lines being delivered as an unseen character.

This text went to press before the end of rehearsals and may differ from the play as performed.

PROLOGUE

'Hot Stuff' by Michael Ball is playing as the audience enter. During which time Alex is inviting people to sit and engaging them in conversation, as he finishes off setting up the room: moving chairs, rolling out plastic sheets, hiding his dirty clothes, moving the cricket bat out of view, etc.

ONE

ALEX *places a phone on the table which he occasionally looks at. He will keep checking this phone intermittently throughout the performance.*

ALEX   Welcome, come in, come in. We might have a few stragglers, but I think we can start. Now, I can see some of our regular faces here, wonderful, great to see you again, hello. So, as you may know, this is actually our tenth bi-annual meeting of the Michael Ball Appreciation Society! #IHeartMichaelBall! For those of you who are new, this is quite the milestone we've reached. 5 years of celebrating the great man himself. I mean, it's amazing, it really is. Now, before I… Actually, I haven't seen you here before, are you local? I'm not asking for a postcode, I'm just researching our online readership.

ALEX *acknowledges any audience member's responses.*

Anyway, before I forget, I've got to say a huge thank you to Dave for choosing tonight's welcome music. You have no idea how fitting it is. I really have dialled about a thousand numbers lately in preparation for tonight. Oh, which reminds me...

ALEX *lifts up a small box from behind the sofa.*

Now, some of you may have one of these already, but in case anyone missed out, to mark the occasion we've got these!

He holds up a small pin badge with 'I Heart MB' on it.

We've got official merch! Now, who hadn't got one? Come on, you don't have one, here. One for you, and you. Put them on.

He hands out the badges to members of the audience and is quite insistent that members put the badges on.

There we go, put them on. Now everyone will know that you were here tonight. That you were a part of something special.

Now... erm... Aimee couldn't make it tonight, I know, I know, before anyone says anything, she knows tonight were gonna be special. I even told her what the plan were, but... well, she seemed to have some issue or something and couldn't make it. So, erm, I've got the minutes from our last meeting, erm, does someone else want to read it with Aimee not being here?

ALEX *offers a piece of paper to members of the audience. If an audience member volunteers, ALEX directs them to the microphone and they read the list into it. If no one volunteers, ALEX reads it himself, but is annoyed that he has to do it.*

ALEX/AUDIENCE (*Reading the minutes*) 19:00. Society members enter to Michael Ball classic, *Love Changes Everything.*

ALEX (*Directly to the audience.*) And I've got to say, we've been through this, all of you who were asking for it again, we can't keep playing the same songs every meeting, alright. Imagine if we were doing a ticketed event, it would cost me a fortune in royalties!

ALEX/AUDIENCE (*Reading the minutes*) 19:10. Meeting commenced by reading previous meetings minutes with nothing to declare.

19:20. Chris gave his rendition of *You Can't Stop The Beat* playing all roles.

ALEX   (*Directly to the audience.*) Bravo for that again, by the way. Bravo. It really was phenomenal.

ALEX/AUDIENCE   (*Reading the minutes*)19:30. List of options for new hashtags on our social media's:
#Michael'sMembers,
#Ball'sBrothers,
#BallLovingBoeBashers,
#MusicalTheatreManiacs,
#Ball'sComingInMyEars,
#BallsDeepOnSundayMorning.

ALEX   (*Directly to the audience*) And I stand by what I said last time, I'm not using those last two. He'll never retweet us with that on them. I really don't think some of you take this society seriously, you know. By the way, if anyone has any more hashtags, feel free to call them out... (*acknowledge, ignore, or move on*).

ALEX/AUDIENCE   (*Reading the minutes*) 19:45. The restraining order against Alex by Alfie Boe.

ALEX   Resolved. Move on. Thank you.

ALEX/AUDIENCE (*Reading the minutes*) 19:50. AOB, none.

          19:55. Close with group rendition of *Empty Chairs at Empty Tables.*

          20:00. Meeting adjourned.

If an audience member has read the minutes, **ALEX** *will indicate that they can sit down again.*

ALEX   Thank you. Which actually brings me quite nicely to today's meeting. Now, I was hoping to play the recording of us singing that Ball classic, but the recording didn't quite work out as I'd have hoped. But, as we all know, that song came out in… come on? When were *Empty Chairs at Empty Tables* released? (*Waits for audience response. This can become a guessing game. Congratulate audiences for getting it right.*) 1985. Well, I didn't hear it until 1999, when I were seven year old. I had no idea it had been around for so long, but then, I guess when you're seven everything's still pretty new. But, even now, the recording sounds so... it sounds as if it were recorded yesterday.

I'm sure we all remember when we first heard his voice, that smooth soulful voice, how about you? When were the first time you heard the voice of an angel? [*This question can be asked to as many audience members as needed. If they don't know, move on.*]

I first heard Michael Ball when I were seven, in the passenger seat of my brother's car. George, that were my brother's name. He'd just passed his test in the November and got this battered old 1986 Citroen AX. The passenger door wouldn't open so I'd always have to slide in from his side. It were meant to be red, but, well some of you may remember the red paint they used to use. By the time George got his hands on it, it were some mix between pink and orange, particularly with the rust around the panels. Anyway, it were coming up to New Years and Mum had got him this cassette tape for Christmas, I didn't know what it were at the time, but George took me out for a drive one evening and he put it on. It started with this robotic telephone voice machine, dialling, old synths, looping around until this slow drum roll, the beat slowly getting its rhythm, the synths playing a really slowed down melody, before suddenly his voice, his voice comes in, smooth and perfect, like a siren calling you to join him, before hitting that first belting note. I were hooked! I mean, you've just heard it, the very track you heard today is the song that started it all. From then on, I wouldn't listen to anything else. We never really had a lot in common growing up, with the age gap and everything, but, that voice brought me and George together. That and cricket actually, we were both into cricket growing up. I've actually still got our old… Anyway, I digress.

GEORGE   I'm gonna sound like him one day.

ALEX   He always used to say that to me. He started to buy up all of Michael's old tapes. The glove box were filled with them. Out of curiosity, what did you listen to growing up? What were playing in your parents cars for example? The music that maybe you hated then, but now gives you a sense of nostalgia. (*Ask audience members directly and strike up conversation where possible, either complimenting or criticising.*) Bob Dylan, Simon and Garfunkel, AC/DC, Shania Twain, The Corrs. We've all got them.

He's from Bromsgrove, you know. That's in Worcestershire. I only learnt that myself last year, the Worcestershire part I mean. I were making some updates on the website when I realised we hadn't included his place of birth. I mean, what were I thinking! How could I forget to include the place of his birth on the actual Michael Ball Appreciation Society webpage!

Just to double check actually, those of you who are new here tonight, do you subscribe to the MBAS page yet? Right, well, if you don't, don't worry about it, we've had to close our website recently for…well, reasons. But, you can still get all your Ball updates on our Twitter @MBAppreciation or on our Facebook, just search for the Michael Ball

Appreciation Society and click follow. Do please also share with your friends and family and help us to build our following, thank you. I know we say no phones during meetings but if you want to quickly do it now, I don't mind. That was Twitter @MBAppreciation or just search Michael Ball Appreciation Society on Facebook. You'll see our logo when you click on it.

ALEX *becomes very pushy towards the audience again, making sure people join the group before he continues.*

He's actually Welsh you know, Michael. On his mother's side. That's why he puts on that silly accent on his radio show sometimes. You can certainly tell there's Welsh blood in him of course, I mean, he can sing for starters! Everyone knows every Welshman can hold a tune. Look at Tom Jones, one hundred and two years old and still belting them out. That's a joke by the way. He's not really a hundred and two... I don't think.

George used to put on this awful Welsh accent when he sang stuff from Phantom. We never had a recording of it with Michael, so he'd do this voice and pretend it was the same thing. He used to do it just to wind me up. I never told him I kind of liked it when he did it though. I always remember it when Michael does it himself on his radio show, makes me think of George every time.

George'd take me out at night in his car for long drives. There were always lots of shouting at home and Dad didn't like it when we played our music, so it were usually the only time we could listen to more than just the one track. Dad were more of an old folk kind of guy. If I came home and The Dubliners, The Blue Horses or The Corries were playing, I knew Dad had already had a few. I used to try and sneak upstairs, but he'd nearly always catch me. I still feel the sting on my legs whenever I hear *The Black Velvet Band*. George would get the same treatment too. There were times when I'd come home from school and see him sat outside the front door. You could tell he'd been crying, and he'd just grab me by the arm and put me in the car.

You know, some people would call Michael Ball guilty pleasure music but it's not. I mean, that implies that I, we, have something to feel bad about. Why should we feel bad for listening to him? If something makes you feel happy, makes you feel safe then what's the harm! I always felt safe being with him, George, and Michael. I mean, if I were with one, I were inevitably with the other.

George used to make mix tapes of Michael's older stuff. Collections of old showtunes and ballads from the early albums, some of them recorded off the radio. We didn't have much money growing up so this were the only way we could keep hearing his voice. We were at home one night, listening to one of these tapes. It must have been selections from Les Mis or something I think, we were both taking turns at the different roles, it were amazing. For all the things we didn't have in common, singing these songs together were just so... It always made Mum smile too, watching us playing all the parts, laughing and giggling.

There is a groaning coming from offstage. **ALEX** *hears it but tries to ignore it.*

Dad came home while we were singing. He'd been to the pub after work. I were still too young to spot the signs, but you could see it in George's eyes, Mum's too, that there were going to be trouble. He stood there for a minute. George had stopped singing but the track were still playing. I didn't know. I kept going. I sang along to Javert's suicide not knowing what fate had in store just minutes later.

DAD   This is all your fault! You gave him that fucking tape! You encouraged him! Look at them! Prancing about like a pair of fucking queers!

ALEX   The slap he gave her. Kept giving her. The sound of a hand hitting skin. Like applause, continuous and never relenting. George tried to stop him, but Dad were too strong, he just threw him to the floor. He kept hitting her, his hands going red. Her eyes going black. He turned to me. He came to me. He pushed his face against mine.

DAD   Sing!

ALEX   His breath stank. His eyes were blood shot and red. His teeth were almost black.

DAD   Fucking sing, now!

ALEX   I froze. I couldn't move. I couldn't think.

DAD   Not so fucking queer now are you.

ALEX   He pushed me to the floor and started to take off his belt. I heard the snap as he folded it on itself. And then there were quiet. Absolute silence, just for a minute. The track were changing on the tape and George were holding Dad's arm. But it didn't last. As the bass strings kicked in from *Empty Chairs*, Dad threw George to the floor once more and beat him so hard that when he'd finished, George just laid there. Red & Black.

The next day the silence were back. There were no more singing. Not the next day, or the next day, or the day after that. Months went by and we didn't even go for a drive anymore. Michael had gone.

Months later, just coming up to Christmas again actually, George told me to come with him to the shops. We got in the car and drove in silence until he pulled up in a car park. I waited for him to move so I could climb out his door, but he just sat there.

GEORGE   I'm leaving.

ALEX   He didn't even look at me. He just stared out of the front window and said it. "I'm leaving."

           I didn't know what he meant. Leaving? I were only eight by this point. I didn't know leaving were even an option.

GEORGE   I'm going down to London and I'm going to be like Michael Ball. I'm going to train, and I'm going to perform on stage, and I'm going to be famous and release records.

ALEX	He finally looked at me.
GEORGE	And as soon as I can afford to, you can come and live with me.
ALEX	I couldn't believe what he were saying. I couldn't imagine George not being there, but I were so excited that I could be living in that London. When George said "soon"... to an eight year old soon ain't long, it's next week, it's tomorrow, it's tea time.
GEORGE	Before I go, I've got a present for you.
ALEX	He gestured to the glove box. I opened it and inside, along with all his tapes were a small paper bag.
GEORGE	Before you open it, you've got to promise me something. Play it every day. Play it every day and sing along and think of me and remember that I'll always look after us.
ALEX	I just nodded again. Inside this paper bag were another tape. The orange and yellow cover of Michael Ball's *This Time... It's Personal* album. We hadn't even listened to Michael in

months, but when we put that cassette in the machine we sang along to every song we knew! *Walking In Memphis, If Tomorrow Never Comes, The First Time Ever I Saw Your Face.* All the great covers, and suddenly this… beautiful ballad came on. Not a cover. An original song. It were ours.

'Just When' by Michael Ball begins to play. **ALEX** *moves to the mic and sings along. After the song, he speaks directly to the audience again.*

I stuck by my promise. I still listen to that album every day, the same cassette and everything. It jumps about a little bit now but… George held up his end too. He went to London straight after Christmas. I'm not sure what he actually told Mum and Dad about where he were going but, he wrote to me, and phoned every now and then. He went and trained in Guildford, the same place Michael trained, to sound just like him.

ALEX *tries to unlock the phone that is on the table. He can't do it. He doesn't have the correct thumb print. He hands the phone*

29

to a member of the audience to hold. He walks offstage. There is a huge scream. **ALEX** *returns with bloodied hands, holding a severed thumb.*

TWO

The groaning continues from offstage. **ALEX** *tries to ignore it but is struggling.*

Before I go on, I feel I need to clarify something, particularly for you newbies. I'm not a creep or a freak or anything like that. I started the Michael Ball Appreciation Society about ten year ago, and I know there are other groups out there but... I set up the Appreciation Society to really help people understand his power, the power of his voice and his voice alone. Michael doesn't need other voices alongside his, he doesn't need duets, he doesn't need partners!

The groaning continues.

Michael is at his best when he is by himself. The passion in his voice. I've felt it, I've sung with that voice all my life. I've sung with Michael in George's car, with George. George's voice would echo Michael's and I would be the only one to sing with him. Only I can sing with him!

ALEX *storms offstage and there is a thudding sound.*

(*Offstage.*) Come here!

The groaning stops. ALEX *returns, snatches the phone back from the audience member and walks over to the table. He unlocks the mobile phone with the severed thumb. Nothing has come through and he looks disappointed.* ALEX *leaves the thumb on the table next to the phone. He returns to the centre of the stage.*

Now, I know I've invited you all here tonight and it's all a bit cloak and dagger...

ALEX *realises he has blood on his hands and finds something to wipe them on.*

...but, I've sort of arranged a bit of a surprise for you all. Now, I don't really want to give too much away just yet because... well, I'm still sort of ironing out the finer details, but... well, trust me, it'll be worth it. I hope. Besides, let's face it, we're all in the same boat really, if you weren't here tonight then you'd only be sat at home watching old clips of Michael online, right? In fact, yeah, that could be a fun game to kill some time. If you weren't here tonight, what would you be doing? Come on? Any takers? You?

ALEX *poses this question to multiple members of the audience, some he may respond positively to, others he may criticise or simply ignore.*

I knew this person once who really liked U2 and would describe Bono's voice as honey running over gravel, which I've got to say makes no sense whatsoever because, I mean, what does honey over gravel even sound like? And why would you even want to pour honey over gravel in the first place? You certainly wouldn't want to eat it, would you? Anyway, to me, Michael's voice is just honey. Pure and simple, unadulterated honey. Why's he going on about honey, you ask? Right? Well, you see, I had this idea when I first set up the Society to use this analogy on the website, so I bought loads of jars of honey and stuck pictures of Michael's face on them, I called it Ball Honey, but I don't think the message were actually all that clear. And the few orders I did get seemed to be from strange men who weren't part of the society. (*Pause*) The t-shirts I designed, on the other hand, did really well though! (*He unzips his cagoul to reveal an 'I Heart MB' t-shirt*) These went like hot cakes when they first came out. I even shipped one to Japan once! He's universally loved that man. I've got some here with me tonight if anyone wants to buy one. I actually have a few of the jars of Ball Honey left too if anyone's interested?

ALEX *rifles around in the box. He pauses.*

Probably a little past their best now though. They didn't used to be set.

He graduated by the way, George, from Guildford. He came home for the weekend after his graduation. We couldn't believe it, me and Mum. Dad obviously didn't care. We hadn't seen him in nearly four years. He pulled up in the same old Citroen AX, even more orange now from the rust.

He came in and Mum and I just wrapped our arms around him, practically squeezing the life out of him. But, when Dad came downstairs, he just walked straight past him and out the door. You'd have thought George had just told him he killed someone or something. In the years that George had been away, Dad hadn't changed, he'd just focused his anger more on me and Mum. If anything, it seemed worse. George used to have to time his phone calls for when he thought Dad might be out, otherwise I'd only get a beating after I hung up. I were 12 year old and there weren't a single part of my body that hadn't been bruised at some point. Other than my face, of course. Couldn't let school find out.

Dad had some of his work friends round once. Five or six of them. All drunk. He put on one of his Dubliners records.

FIRST DRUNK Where's your eldest these days?

ALEX   They always asked after George when they came round. They didn't actually care; I think they just liked to tease Dad about his singing.

DAD   Dead.

35

ALEX   He were already slurring his words from the
            drink. I corrected him, not knowing better, and
            said he'd moved down to London to be a singer
            like Michael Ball. His hand came down on me
            so hard.

            I thought one of his friends might help me, but
            they all just laughed.

SECOND DRUNK I gave our Thomas a black eye last week
            for back chatting me.

THIRD DRUNK That's nothing, mine's got a fractured
            elbow. That'll learn him not to forget to the put
            the dog out before bed.

ALEX   These drunken old men, trying to one up each
            other with the pain and abuse they inflicted on
            their own children.

DAD   You hear that, Alex. Think yourself lucky I'm
            so soft on you.

ALEX   Suddenly, *The Irish Rover* began to play on the
            record. A cheer shook the room, as they all
            jumped up. I were pushed to the ground as they
            all began chanting along. When it came to the

verse sung by The Pogues though, it began. Dad picked me up and knocked me across the room with his fists and with each count they all took a hit. "One million bags... two million barrels... three million sides... four million barrels of bones."

I never told George about it when he phoned that week.

Anyway, where was I? That's right. So, George had come home, and he asked if I wanted to go for a drive, like old times. Ask a dumb question, right? The passenger door still didn't work, and the engine were starting to make this weird whirring, scraping sort of sound, even when it weren't moving. I did notice one new addition to the car though. He'd got this weird plug-in adaptor thing so he could play CDs in it rather than just his old tapes.

GEORGE   Old thing kept chewing them up. This thing's great, it'll never damage your music again.

ALEX   With that, he hit play and on it came. An oldie but a classic. *Love Changes Everything*. 2004 were the release of *Love Changes Everything: The Essential Michael Ball*. And I've got to say, everything on that album were essential. You've got to remember that the internet in 2004 weren't the internet of today. Half of these songs I'd never heard before. There were covers here I'd never even dreamed of. And there were one on there that were very special to me. George paused it after track six and looked at me.

GEORGE   1992 were when you were born, weren't it?

ALEX   He knew fine well.

GEORGE   Also in 1992, Michael Ball represented the UK in Eurovision. Came second he did. Only beaten by Ireland.

ALEX   I had no idea! Did you? I mean, you might know now, but I certainly didn't know then! *One Step Out of Time*. (*A short clip of 'One Step Out of Time' plays before cutting off*) Best song for dancing to… EVER!! Particularly the live version! Absolute banger that!

Anyway, George had some news to tell me. He said that in your final term at Guildford, they encourage you to go out and audition so when you've graduated you can get straight into work. George had been doing this and he'd got a job! Now you've got to remember, George went to Guildford to train like Michael Ball, to sound like Michael Ball, so what were the first job he went and got? He got Marius in Les Misérables! Michael Ball's first leading role! I couldn't believe it. I couldn't have been happier for him. It were just a small production he said, but it were still paid work. A few more tracks into the album and we got to *that* Les Mis song and my god. I don't know what they teach at Guildford, but they'd done it. He sounded just like Michael. I were now sat in the car with Michael Ball, singing *Empty Chairs at Empty Tables* together! George and Michael were suddenly one and the same. Their voices, indistinguishable.

GEORGE   The plan's working. It won't be long before you can come and live with me. Few more roles under my belt and I'll have a place of my own, then I'll send for you.

ALEX   George weren't home long before he had to head back down south. I missed him every day. But I knew one day we could be together. Whenever Dad went out, I put on one of Michael's tapes and I sang along as if it were George there with me.

The groaning sound returns from offstage along with some thudding. The groaning sounds different this time in some way.

Excuse me.

ALEX *walks off stage.*

Right!

A struggle can be heard offstage consisting of non-descript swearing and retaliation. The mobile phone, which is still on the table, finally sounds. **ALEX** *returns to the stage carrying a bloodied cricket bat and also with a lot of blood on his 'I Heart MB' t-shirt. There will be no more noise from the other room. He rushes straight to the phone to read the message. He looks a little annoyed by the message.* **ALEX** *thinks for a moment, suddenly gets an idea and replies.*

That should do it.

He puts the phone back on the table.

THREE

ALEX A couple more years went by. 2007. *Hairspray.* (*A single beep sounds.* **ALEX** *doesn't hear it.*) George had had a few more jobs after Les Mis. He'd even done some small touring productions, but it were in 2007 that it finally happened. Michael Ball were playing Edna Turnblad in a new production of *Hairspray* at the Shaftsbury Theatre in London and George had got the role of understudy... (*A single beep sounds again.*) understudy for Michael Ball! Not bad for someone half his age. He'd finally made it.

This were going to be it, the big break that meant I could live with him. (*Beep.*) He must have been so excited. I can only imagine how he must have felt when he got that call. He called me straight after. (*Beep.*) I couldn't believe it. He said it would only be another month or so and then I could go and live with him! (*Beep.*) I started to pack. How he must have felt on that first morning of rehearsals when he woke up. (*Beep*) I told Mum I were

42

leaving to live with him. (*Beep.*) How the
adrenaline must have been (*Beep.*) rushing
through his body as he left for the rehearsal
(*Beep.*) I told Dad I hated him (*Beep.*) and that
I never wanted to see him again! (*Beep.*) George
were so excited (*Beep.*) he ran across the road
to get to the studio... (*Beep.*) when a taxi hit
him.

There is a long sustained beep. Silence.

I bet he were barely one step out of time.

Silence.

That were 15 year ago. 15 year today. To think
George were so close to not just singing with
Michael but being good enough to be a backup
Michael. To *be* Michael Ball. All those times I
were singing with George in the car, and I were
singing with Michael.

One reason I wanted to bring you all here today
weren't only to celebrate Michael Ball, but to
join me in remembering my brother. Like
many of you, I'm sure, I recently bought

Michael's latest album and there's a song on there I just really wanted to share with you. I hope you don't mind.

'Never Let You Go' by Michael Ball begins to play. **ALEX** *sings along. There is a silence after the song.* **ALEX** *composes himself.*

When I turned 18, I tried out at Guildford myself. I didn't get in. I tried out for loads of those drama school places. None of them took me. Seems I weren't meant to follow in Michael or George's footsteps. I ended up just going to a Uni in Wales. Weren't really where I wanted to go but I thought, if I could at least pick up the accent, maybe I'd be able to sing like Michael then. Plus I needed to go somewhere to get away from home. Dad's drinking had got worse, and Mum had become even more complacent with it. I couldn't be there anymore.

I got kicked out of Uni at Christmas, well, sort of. I started a fight with the Musical Theatre Lecturer… apparently. He asked who everyone's favourite singers and performers were. I said Michael Ball, and he shook his head. "Too much vibrato for me," he said. "Shows a lack of control. I prefer John Owen Jones personally." I can't really say I remember much more after that. The Uni said that if I promised to leave straight away and not come back next term then they wouldn't see the need to press any charges. Personally I think the head of department were actually on my side about the whole thing, but obviously she couldn't admit to that in front of the other lecturers. Solidarity at work and all that. I sent her a t-shirt after I'd got settled back in at home, with a letter thanking her for her support.

I started volunteering after Uni. The Shooting Star Children's Hospice. I tend to take my CDs with me and play them some music for a bit. Maybe dance and sing along. (*Pause*) Michael's a patron there, you know, has been since 2009. I'm thinking that if I keep going every day and playing his music then maybe one day I'll get to meet him. I've been going there for about ten year now. Apparently I always just miss him. Did you know that in 2012, for his 50th birthday, he told people not to get him any presents but instead we should just give money to the charity? (*Pause*) How lovely is that? He's practically a saint. I bet he'd do anything for that charity. Even a last minute benefit gig if you told him it would help the children. (Alex *smiles*.) If he thought there were a child sat at home, sat in this home maybe? Desperate to hear his voice one last time, as his one dying wish, I bet he'd come running.

The phone pings once more. **ALEX** *becomes very excited but tries to calm himself before he reads the message. He freezes, staring at the phone in disbelief.*

2016, things got serious. As a lot of you will know, Michael has always been happy to do duets with some of the greats of the theatre world, but in 2016 things took a turn. Sure, 2016 brought us Brexit, 2016 brought us Trump. But, 2016 brought us *him*. Michael is a solo performer, always has been, but in 2016 *he* came along. He jumped into Michael's shadow and highjacked everything he had worked so hard for. You all know who I'm talking about. Like a tiny, bearded leech, clinging on to Michael's success. Decades of training, working, developing, honing his skills, his talents, his charisma. And he thinks he can just swoop in! Sat next to him, singing along to the songs Michael had already made his own. Michael Ball takes other people's songs and makes them better, he takes good songs and makes them great, great songs and makes them amazing, amazing songs and makes them outstanding. He is perfection. Sat in that car, singing with him. Singing along to Michael's hits in his old Citroen AX. I should be singing with him. I should be singing with George not Alfie fucking Boe!

Together, *Back Together*, *Together Again*, *Together at Christmas*, and now, *Together this Summer!* Well, we'll see about that, won't we. #AllBallNoBoe.

ALEX *frantically picks up the phone and begins typing a reply. He sends the message and watches the screen.*

> You see, *this* is why I called you here tonight. Tonight. The anniversary of my brother's death. The anniversary of the night my brother should have stood next to Michael Ball. The night he should have sung with him, been him, made it so that I could have been singing with him. Well, tonight we shall all sing with him. You see, Mr Boe, is surprisingly easy to get a hold of. Literally. Easy to get a hold of, tie up, gag and throw into the back of an old Citroen AX. And if anyone is going to have the contact details for Michael Ball, it's Boe.

The phone pings again.

> He's coming. He's coming!

ALEX *throws the phone down and starts moving around, excited, and unsure of his own movements.*

> He's coming! He's coming! Oh my god he's coming. Oh my god, I'm going to be sick. He's

actually on his way. He's actually... Oh my god, he's on his way. Now. Shit!

ALEX *tries to compose himself. He acts out various 'hello' scenarios and practices how he will stand before realising the state of the room.* ALEX *encourages members of the audience to help him tidy up before he realises what he is wearing.*

Shit!

ALEX *instructs the audience members back to their seats and, moving frantically again, he looks desperately for something to change into before remembering who is offstage.* ALEX *goes off stage and returns moments later in a shirt and blazer.*

Well, I think it's safe to say you're not going to need it anymore, eh Alfie?

Ok George. One more song. Just one more song. That's all I need. To be back in that car. Back together.

Blackout. There is a knock at the door.

EPILOGUE

*Lights come up, colourful and flashing like a disco. As the audience exit, 'One Step Out Of Time' by Michael Ball plays and **ALEX** sings along, encouraging the audience to join in.*

Blackout.

THE END

YES

Alexander Millington

Yes was first performed at The Shop Front Theatre, Coventry on 9 May 2019, as part of New Project Theatre's *Confessions* showcase with the following cast:

DAVID   James Will

Director   Charlie Ingram

CHARACTERS

David, *male, middle-aged*

DAVID *is sitting, smiling to himself. He is professionally dressed yet relaxed.*

DAVID It would have been 1985 that I decided. I wasn't rushing it, I wasn't being impulsive, I just knew that I was ready, that we were ready. It was what we both wanted. We weren't naïve, at least, I didn't think I was. I'd had my experiences of the world, I'd had some fun, I'd lived a little. But, at that moment everything just felt right. We'd talked about it, as you do when you're young, but never seriously, just little things like what we'd have at the buffet and what we'd name our children, if we even wanted children or would we be one of those couples who just have pets. We wanted both. We were both raised with pets; hers always dogs and mine always had chickens, and both of us had come from big families.

I did the proper thing, I asked her father first, nice and traditional. Particularly as her father would most likely be paying. It would have been rude of me not to ask really. Asking him, as was the case when asking her, was like what I imagine falling off a tall building would be like. It just went on and on, it felt like hours passing, you could see their face change with the thought process as you would see the pavement coming towards your nose. Then the answer came and went, and I felt as if I barely heard it: "Yes."

There was no doubt about who was to be my best man. That was even more of a cliché than the ceremony itself. Best friends since school, holidayed together, rugby together, even fell out over girls together before realising neither of us even wanted them, but that's boys. Boys will be boys. He did what any best mate does when a bloke says he's popping the question: "Are you sure you're ready? You're still young, you've got your whole life ahead of you. Ahh… but if you're happy… Congratulations!" That look of: you're about to ruin your life, before realising it's meant to be a good thing. To be fair to him, he was always the same way at school, that caution before just throwing himself into it, giving in to the joy of it. Sometimes just throwing yourself into something can lead to your most memorable experiences. That was always our motto. Just saying yes instead of no, just once, can change your life.

One thing I didn't realise, or at least didn't think about, was the meetings with the vicar. When you meet them, after you've got to know each other a little bit and that nervous tension has gone, they ask you these questions, they actually have to, it's a thing. "What are her favourite films, his music, her colour, his meals? Where did the two of you meet? What do you both hope for the future? What do you think will change afterwards?" As if we were doing it for some scam you know, get myself a visa or something. Then I suppose it's not uncommon really is it? But it was the last one that got me though: "What do I think will change?" What would change? We'd obviously start living together, probably open a joint account, start thinking about a mortgage after we get tired of paying rent. We'd have to talk about our wills, pensions, savings, debts. Whether we want to be in a house or a bungalow, how will we decorate, we'll need to get colour charts, dust sheets, paint tins, overalls. What if we can't agree on a colour? Will that be the start of something? The small things that lead to the big things that keep you up at night. What is going to change?

I suddenly notice her hand on top of mine. "Nothing," she told the vicar. "Things are going to stay exactly as they are." I turned to see her looking at me, smiling at me. "Good," they said. They went on to talk about all the people that suddenly expect everything to become a fairy-tale, "when really nothing will change at all."

After that particular clerical visit I couldn't help thinking about all the things that would actually change afterwards. I didn't tell her of course, I didn't want to worry her, thinking I was getting cold feet or anything. We used to tell each other everything. Every detail of our days, every thought in our heads, everything we wanted for the future and everything that had been in our past. But I knew I couldn't share these thoughts with her. No matter how much I loved her, because I loved her. Sometimes you just need to keep things to yourself.

DAVID begins to relax a little more, takes off his jacket, possibly, if he has one or removes his tie and rolls it up.

So, the day came. Needless to say she looks stunning. Both her parents dressed up to the nines, her mother, glamourous as ever. My parents, dressed nice for them. My father in his best Sunday suit, a suit that has heard more Catholic prayers and sermons than the Pope's mitre. And my mother, in a dress that, if it was any darker, would have looked fitting for a funeral. Thankfully both sets of parents got on and always managed to make pleasant conversation, we were thankful for that of course, particularly as no one ever managed to maintain conversation, pleasant or otherwise, with my mother. When I told her of my intentions, whereas my father hugged me and congratulated me, she simply said "Well, I suppose at least it'll stop you hanging around with those friends of yours quite so much". *Those friends*, referring to one friend, my best friend, whom she had no reason to dislike other than the fact she disliked everyone. It's not as if she ever saw us doing anything she wouldn't approve of, but maybe that's just because boys are good at hiding things from their mothers.

As I watched my soon- to- be walk down the aisle towards me, her father on her arm walking with military precision, I felt my best man's hand on my back, supporting me as ever through any big decision. As I looked at him, I saw a tear in his eyes. We'd gone through so much together. As my soon-to-be father-in-law approached to give his daughter away, I felt as if it was my friend who was giving me away, releasing me.

There is a long silence **DAVID** *remembers the day. He smiles but at times looks sad.*

We got a house, rented first of course, but within the first couple of years we managed to scrape enough together for that deposit, with a little help from her father, of course. We even got the pets, dogs, just one to start with but it wasn't long before we thought a second would provide good company. It was one of those decisions we didn't even really need to make, like when you go to Maccies and they ask if you want fries, "yes", or salt and vinegar on chips, "yes". Did we want to have our own home with loving dogs, "yes". Did we want to get pregnant before we could really afford a full family, maybe not. Another conversation where your nose is getting close to the pavement, but this time you remember the painful feeling. But you learn to adapt. You don't spend quite as much money on take-aways, you don't go out to the pub every week, you find a more fuel-efficient, family car, you don't feel in the mood to have sex together anymore. That was a hard one to adapt to. Suddenly saying "yes" wasn't the likely option. "No" became quite the frequent answer, from both of us. We both wanted to want to, but neither of us ever did. We asked the doctor about it and apparently it's quite normal, the woman is naturally exhausted from everything her body is putting her through and the man just loses interest, either from giving up after so many rejections or unfortunately due to the bump. In her defence though, she still looked beautiful as ever, even with the bump, we'd just drifted apart at some point over the nine months. The honeymoon period was over.

I helped her whenever I could to make the pregnancy easier, hot water bottles, making meals, massages. I'm not saying I was perfect, I could tell when I was getting on her nerves, usually because I was being *too* supportive. You forget that sometimes the best thing to do is just leave her alone for a moment. So, I left her alone. Whenever I felt I was getting in the way I'd refill her waterbottle and head out for a couple of hours, give her the space she wanted. I started going to the gym, started going a lot, particularly toward the end of the pregnancy. I used to meet my best man, it was a little like old times. When we used to play rugby together it was always a laugh, the two of us always grabbing at each other, teasing and roughing each other up a little. We'd grown up now of course but once we got in that gym the competitive side came back in both of us. The treadmills, the weights, the rowing machine. Our bodies just sweating as we pushed ourselves. The gloves were always off when it was the two of us.

Back on the field we used to set each other forfeits for the one who scored the least tries. Stupid stuff like streaking across the pitch or trying to pull the coach's daughter. This time though the forfeits were harder to think of. We had to be adults now, had to keep things smaller scale, didn't want to lose our memberships.

"First one to get to 7K on the treadmill gets his body washed by the loser!" he called out. Both of us quickly picking up the pace, him being slightly ahead of me, "haven't had a personal wash since I had my appendix out" I call to him, "hope your hands are gonna be warmer than those nurses!" The talk continues as we reach five k, five and a half, six. It's gonna be close, we're literally just metres apart. Six and a half. Six point seven, point eight, nine…

That night he came. Nine pounds, seven ounces, our first child, our son. One of the attendants at the gym came and found us in the changing room to let me know there had been a call for me. I made it to the hospital just in time to see him be born. If it was any other person's child I'd describe it as a screaming, chubby, wrinkly, little pink thing, covered in I don't even want to know what. But this was mine, this was ours, he was beautiful. The thing

I really remember most about him is how dark his eyes were, as if he had something hidden behind them, as if he already had a secret to hide.

Of course, with the baby now with us I had to be even more hands on, and believe me I wanted to be, I was more than happy to do anything and everything I could to spend time with him. To tell you the truth I think she was happy to see the back of him a little bit too. After all, nine months of having something constantly leeching off all your nutrients, weighing you down, you'd be glad to be shot of it too. And I was happy to take over. I was a good dad.

He pauses for a moment, staring out. Through the next section **DAVID** *slowly and methodically unties and removes his shoes followed by his socks which he folds up and tucks into his shoes.*

Only after a child do you really start to know the difference between growing up and growing old. Over ten years you see your child go from the small, wrinkly, pink mess, to a smiling little crawler who chews on things to investigate, through being a crier, to a laugher, to a talker. You watch as they become aware of shapes and objects to the point where they can then draw them from memory, to being able to read and write and tell stories. They understand conversation, they understand questions and answers, they know right from wrong, good from evil, yes from no. For someone who has already grown up though, growing old is all you have left. I watched my wife's face, as the wrinkles started to appear and the pinkness leave her cheeks. The crow's feet and greys hairs materialise as the body begins to creek and groan. As my own body starts to ache and the mere thought of intimacy together is enough to give you a stitch. Over the ten years I had loved watching my son grow up, I had felt proud watching him develop into who he wanted to be. My wife and I might have stopped being intimate quite so much, but for what we had gained, it was worth it.

You hear people say that having kids changes your life forever and it's true, but it's not the lack of sleep or lack of money or privacy that comes straight to my mind as it does for others. That never bothered me. The biggest impact our little boy has had on me is I no longer know how to walk down the street without feeling his hand in mine. I can't drive anywhere without seeing him in my mirror, sat there, smiling away on the back seat. Eating a meal or watching TV and not hearing his laugh somewhere in the house, reminding me that no matter how bad a day I've had, it doesn't matter. I can't imagine my life without him.

I walk slower now. These past years of walking along with him by my side, making sure I'm not walking too fast for him, means I can no longer walk as fast as a normal human being, even when he's not with me. I've become one of those people you dread getting stuck behind on the high street cause I can't stop dawdling. I used to think it won't be long before he's pulling me along down the street, or simply overtake me. These are the little things you don't realise, you don't think about. All those chats you had about whether or not to have children, not once did either of us think, "well it's going to slow us down when we go into town". These are the little things, the things that make the real changes in your life.

Our son now at secondary school, my wife working full time again, I'd even managed to get some promotions over the past years and was doing quite well at work now, but the life was draining from me. I needed to feel alive again. I used to lay awake each night trying to remember when it was I really felt invigorated and energetic and happy. I realised it was the night he was born, the night I became a father. But it wasn't that that made me feel alive. It was being at the gym.

A couple of months ago, I signed back up. Started going quite regularly, I was surprised how easy it was for me to get back into the swing of it. After a couple weeks though I didn't feel any different, no more alive or full of energy, because it wasn't the actual gym that made me feel that way.

It had been a few years since we last spoke, but I still recognised his voice when I called. He's similar to me now. Married, got a kid, he's got a daughter. He asked if I wanted to meet up for a drink, of course I said "yes". We met up at our old local from when we were young, a little out of town but I told her not to wait up. She knew what we were like when we got together, never just a quick drink and then home. We spent most of the night just talking, asking questions and learning about each other's new lives. I asked him if he remembered the night my son was born. He said "yes". I asked him if he remembered exactly what happened the night he was born. He said "yes". I asked him if he still thought about it. He said "yes". When he asked me the same in return I couldn't say no. When he asked me if I thought about it a lot, I couldn't say no. And when he asked if I wanted to go upstairs with him...

I didn't go with the intention... If he hadn't asked I wouldn't have gone up. I wouldn't have asked, I wouldn't have done that to him, I wouldn't. But he did. He asked me. He knew I'd say yes. I wish he didn't ask. I wish I didn't say yes.

DAVID *stands up from his seat, he appears tense for the first time.*

When I told her... When I told her, our son was asleep in the next room. You could see on her face the struggle she was having to not scream as she cried. I can't bear the thought of her looking at me like that again. I don't want her to hate me. I don't want my son to hate me. She asked why, and I couldn't answer. When she asked if I still loved her, I couldn't answer.

A mobile phone rings from within **DAVID's** *pocket. He gets it out, he is on the verge of tears. He does not answer. He places the phone down on the floor next to him.*

I'm sorry.

DAVID *jumps. There is an instant blackout. The sound of a person screaming is heard as if from below. The phone rings again as a crowd can be heard. Fade to silence.*

THE END

OVER TIME

Alexander Millington

Over Time was first released on BBC Sounds on 13 July 2020 ahead of its broadcast on BBC Radio on 21 July 2020 with the following cast:

VERA   Sheila Mumby

Director   Alexander Millington

CHARACTERS

Vera, *female, elderly*

VERA *is seated at her kitchen table in her dressing gown. She has a cup of coffee in front of her. She puts her hand over the top of the coffee mug for a moment, feeling the heat from the steam. She takes her hand away, looks at the mug for a moment, then clasps both hands around it. There is a chair opposite her at the table. See looks at it as if there is someone there.*

VERA   Do you remember that blackout we had in '84? I think it was then that I knew. There was something in the way you looked at me, something in your eyes that night.

We sat here, at this table, it must have been not long after we moved in actually. I'd just managed to get dinner sorted before the lights went. I want to say we had fish fingers; I seem to remember us eating a lot of fish fingers when we first moved in. You'd spent all day getting the freezer plugged in and stocked up, I'd set the table and cooked the fish fingers and… POP! Out went the lights, off went the radio, and of course, off went the freezer too. (*She laughs to herself.*) "Bloody hell it's gone kaput!" You still felt uncomfortable swearing in front of me. Thirty years later you still don't really swear in front of me. I know you do though, when you're out

72

with Mike and everyone, you think I don't know, but I do. "Bloody hell it's all gonna be ruined!" I told you it would be fine though, just leave the lid down and keep the cool air in, it'll soon pass.

You lit the candles and I plated up. You used the flame of the candles to warm your knife so you could spread your butter smoothly on the bread, I remember.

Halfway through the meal, I looked up from my plate and saw you looking at me. Staring. It was as if you were staring straight through me, piercing me with your eyes. I know it might have been a little late in the day, being as we had already married and moved in together but that was when I knew, really knew, that I was going to be with you forever. (*Her tone deepens.*) But, then again, maybe it was just the candlelight.

I'm sure it was no coincidence that it was nine months after that night that Susanne came along. (*Smiling again.*) You always said you never wanted a child, that you'd never make a good father. "How could I ever love something that's gonna bleed us dry," you always used to say. Even in the hospital you didn't want to hold her. I heard the nurse offer her to you while I was resting, you must have thought I was asleep. "I don't wanna touch it," you said. "I don't wanna touch it." You thought I never heard you, but I did. That's why, when we got back home, the first thing I did was go out and leave her with you. I knew if I left the two of you alone for a bit, you'd soon warm to her.

When I came home, I could just see the back of your head over the top of the chair. You'd fallen asleep. I was about to go ballistic at you for nodding off when you should have been looking after Susie, but as I came round the chair I saw her, cradled in your arms, both of you fast asleep. You never knew that I saw that, but I did.

I could never accuse you of not providing for us, of not looking after us. Every time they offered you extra work, you took it. "We need the money." And you were right, we did. And you always made sure we got it. It just would have been nice to have had a few more weekends together, a few more evenings as the three of us. Rather than me looking after everything and just plating up your tea for when you got home. But you always made sure we had plenty. I did know that.

Even after Susie went off to University you kept taking the extra time. I told you we didn't need it anymore; Susie even had her own job by then. "You never know though, things change. Better to have too much than too little." And you were right of course.

I got a phone call once, from your work. It was sometime around our anniversary; I forget which one now. They were asking after you, of course they didn't want me, wanting to know if you wanted some extra hours. They said they wouldn't normally bother you because they knew you weren't ever interested in the extra time but, they were desperate. They meant to ask before you left at five, but they missed you. I said I thought you were still there. They said "no". (*She considers.*) I laughed it off and said I must have got my days mixed up. When you came home and I asked how your day was, you said "long". You gave me an entire account of your day. I never told you I'd had that phone call, never told you I knew about the extra time, never told you that I cried that night, but I did.

You kept working your extras; late nights, Saturday mornings. I stopped asking how your day had been. I just got tired of hearing the lies. I often wondered if you ever noticed?

When that woman came round today, after the service, I didn't even think to ask who she was. I just let her in. She began telling me how sorry she was for my loss, how upset she was, and that she was sorry to have tell me like this. "Tell me what?" I asked her.

You thought I didn't know.

THE END